Y0-DBZ-545

The Reason for Nasturtiums

811.54
D641

The Reason for Nasturtiums

Chitra Banerjee Divakaruni

B·P·W·P
BERKELEY
· POETS ·
WORKSHOP
& PRESS
P.O. Box 459
Berkeley, CA 94701

ACKNOWLEDGEMENTS

Some of these poems have appeared in the following publications: *Amelia, Beloit Poetry Journal, Berkeley Poets Coop, Buffalo Spree, Calapooya Collage, Chelsea, Embers, Floating Island, Hurricane Alice, In the Via Gombito, an Anthology,* New Rivers Press, *India Currents, Indiana Review, Kalliope, The Literary Review, Occident, and Z Miscellaneous.*

The author wishes to thank the Santa Clara Arts Council for its generous grant which helped to make this book possible.

Copyright © 1990 Chitra Divakaruni.
All rights reserved.

Berkeley Poets Workshop & Press
P.O. Box 459
Berkeley, California 94701

ISBN #0-917658-28-0

Cover design by author with the help of Foothill College Graphics and Foothill College Teaching Resource Center.

Typeset and Design by Typesetting Etc., San Francisco, California.
Printed by Braun-Brumfield, Inc., Ann Arbor, Michigan.

CONTENTS

once
more
for
Murthy

The Reason for Nasturtiums

I

THE NISHI

Sometimes I wake up suddenly with the blood hammering in my chest and hear it, a voice I can't quite place, deep inside the tunnel of my ear, tiny, calling my name, pulling out the syllables like threads of spun-sugar, *Chit-ra, Chit-ra.*

ii

When I was very little, my mother used to sing me to sleep. Or tell me stories. A jewel was stitched to the end of each, and when her voice reached that place, it took on a shivering, like moonlit water.

iii

Some nights I woke to hear her through the thin bedroom wall. *Not tonight, please, not tonight.* Shuffles, thuds, panting, then a sharp cry, like a caught bird's. I would burrow into the pillow that smelt of stale lint and hair oil, squeeze shut my eyes so red slashes appeared, hold my breath till all I heard was the roaring in my ears.

iv

After father left her she rarely spoke above a whisper. *Go to the closet under the stairs,* she would say, very soft. *I don't want to see your face.* Her voice was a black well. If I fell into it, I would never find my way out. So the closet, with its dry, raspy sounds, a light papery feel like fingers brushing against my leg, making me pee in my pants.

v

What do you do when the dark presses against your mouth, a huge clammy hand to stop your crying? What do you do when the voice has filled the insides of your skull like a soaked sponge?

vi

Late at night she would come and get me, pick up my dazed body and hug me to her, pee and all. *I'm sorry, baby, so sorry, so sorry.* Feather kisses down the tracks of dried tears. But perhaps I am dreaming this. Even in the dream she doesn't say *this won't ever happen again.*

vii

I will never have children. Because I have no dark closets in my house, because I don't sing, because I cannot remember any of my mother's stories. Except one.

viii

That night she took out the harmonium, the first time since father left. It was covered in cobwebs, but she didn't dust them away. They clung to her fingers as she played. She let me stay and listen. Outside, a storm. When the thunder came, she let me hide my face in her lap. She was singing love songs. She sang for hours, till her voice cracked. Then she told me the tale of the *Nishi.* She held me till I slept, and when she put me to bed, she locked me in. It was an act of kindness, I think, so I would not be the first to discover her body hanging from the ceiling of the bedroom that was now hers alone.

ix

The Nishi, said my mother, *are the spirits of those who die violent deaths. They come to you at night and call your name in the voice you love most. But you must never answer them, for if you do, they suck away your soul.*

x

Sometimes I wake up, blood hammering, hear it, a voice, deep inside a tunnel, tiny, pulling out the syllables, *Chit-ra, Chit-ra.* And I answer, calling her, wanting to be taken, but nothing happens except the sound of her name webs me in unbreakable threads of spun-sugar.

16

THE DRIVE

Our first evening in Italy and we're careening down Via Appia Antica in Uncle's rickety Fiat, the windows down, the hot July air flooding our skulls with the smell of field dust and manure and drying sunflowers and the crickets crying in the grasses. Uncle aims for the center of every pothole. The car lurches and shudders and Aunt, sitting in front, shrinks into the worn plush of her seat and clutches at her face. Your fingers are gripping the armrest, white, but floating in the last of the brassy light I note them only vaguely. *A Celebration,* Uncle yells, *because it's the first time you and your husband are visiting Rome and me!* Yes, yes, I call out. The signs stream past us, Catacombe di Domitilla, Tomba di Cecilia Metella, a few olive trees with sparse silver leaves, large empty fields of barbed wire, exposed bricks, ruins of pillars, towers, the gates of a hidden villa.

Uncle points. *See where the armies marched in triumph.* Yes, yes. And it is a night with sudden fireflies exploding against the windshield, the sweat-sour smell of old wine drifting through the car like a suspicion, the car going too fast, flying through the potholes and years, is it forward or back, someone crying in the front seat, and your voice with the shaking in it saying shouldn't we be returning to the city. Breathing is hard and wonderful. And it's my father's voice now, rising like bells out of a lost time. *Imagine the emperors at the head of the procession, Augustus and Trajan and Nero.* Yes, yes. The road slippery as a snake twisting trying to throw us off and alien stars hurtling across the inky sky just as in my childhood. So I am ready when the tree looms up, a mad lunge of thorns straight at us, ready this time and laughing above the screams. Is it Aunt or my mother? Ready for the jagged glass, the black splatter of blood, yes, yes, the ambulance's red whirling eye, the pale slits of mouths at the funeral, the relatives saying *we knew, sooner or later, this would happen.*

The brakes screech, the car jerks, I fall forward, hit my forehead, it doesn't hurt, I'm still laughing in great gasps that can't be stopped. You make a harsh sound in your throat and slap me across the mouth. What are *you* doing here, in this car out of my childhood? Thorns scrape metal as you throw the door open and pull Uncle from the driver's seat. Aunt is bent over, crying soundlessly. I want to touch the thin ridges of her shoulder bones, but where are my hands? You shift the gears, reversing, getting us back onto the road, towards the city, away from the fireflies, the past. I read the short stiff hairs on the back of your neck. It's going to be one of those nights. Then he leans towards me, a conspirator, his breath sweet and grape-red, my father's. *Remember the gladiators with their shining tridents, the slaves and Christians naked in chains, behind the chariots the wild caged bears.* Yes, yes, I whisper back.

CHILDHOOD

It was a place where apples sprouted teeth,
the wild duck father shot in the Fall
hung neck down in its purple pimpled skin.
A place where stacked blocks of dark
toppled at the wrong password, where
all the wooden arrows you aimed
quivering and comet-tailed at enormous suns
reappeared flecked with red. And the dreams—
were they always of crows with obsidian beaks,
palmyra trees that turned to tongues or wounds,
and under that twisted judas vine
on your way each day to the yellow school bus
the hunchbacked beggar woman with iron hair
and how you knew you couldn't say no
if she opened the bloated sack of her body
and invited you in.

FOR EVER

    with your white
chest   mottling as we
    oh
and the bones of your back
loose
    this afternoon
of the green mail van
        the tug
and schoolchildren
      who chant
numbers that line up
on stiff legs
      like birds
the small raised moles
    on your shoulder   your
wisteria fingers
       tongue
   and mostly

in the sunny wind
the tarp on a neighbor's roof
flapping like the wild
      wing
   caught inside your skin

THIS SMALL HEAT

Because you are coming from America
after ten years, I set out
a gardenia in a red clay bowl
on the sill against the steel-grey
swell of monsoon. On the radio
Vilayat Khan plays the sitar:
Megh Mallar, a raga
for rain. And I must
push through wet curtains
to the balcony, to the sky where
the warm dark drops mingle
with the winglights
of your plane. Or is it
a moving star? Are you awake?
Are you watching, from your window's
oval, the streetlamps come on
one by one in the city
of your birth? The wind shakes
pungence from the hard green
of mango buds. Rain in my eyes.
Do you feel this small heat,
this opening like a fist
uncurling to fingertips,
this black gardenia
uncurling about us
petal on lightning petal?

OUTSIDE PISA

Above the Boca del Arno the sky
bleeds its last red. The sea gives up
its colors to the dark. On the barren shore
we stand trying to hold hands,
to smile like lovers. The fishermen
have left their nets and poles, black and jagged
against the night's coming. Nothing
left for us to say. Smell of salt
and death, older than this broken harbor, older
than the white tower
this morning by the cathedral.

After all the pictures, how small it seemed,
how fragile in its leaning. Dark slits of stairs,
the sooty upturned spiral, the holding on,
walls damp and slippery to the palm,
surface-scratched with names and hopes:
*Lorenzo e Rosa, Pietro, Clementina, Sally
loves Bill.* And when we came out
into the hot light, all around us
the breathless rainbow sheen of pigeon wings,
couples kissing, mouth to moist
rose-mouth. This same death-smell.
The floor tilted away
from my feet. No railings, just
the adrenalin rush of white edge
into nothing. You were taking pictures. I
kept my face turned away. In case
you saw my eyes, my longing to jump.

When the doctor said
I couldn't have children, I sensed
the stiffening in your bones. We never
spoke of it. Deep
bell-sounds from the baptistry
where they say Galileo discovered
the centripetal motion of this world,
the headlong, wheeling planets held

arc upon arc, calm and enormous,
without accident.
Now I let go your stranger's hand,
the unfamiliar callus on your thumb.
We are suspended as dust
in this dark river air, floating
away from each other, from the other shore
where we cannot be,
its gleam of fairy lights
that we would die for.

EACH NIGHT

After it is over
his breath thickens into sleep.
Pinned under his damp arm
she closes dry eyes.

And stands on the bridge
watching the water,
brackish brown
laden with anemones.

Feels the whirr of gnats
against their petals, against
her hand. Her fingers reach
for the largest anemone,
tip out the water.

Sliding into the stream
she swells like a rotting branch
and watches the thickening green
close over her head.

Her eyes are pebbles, smooth and slippery
in stagnant water.
Somewhere a submarine light
distends the underneath of an anemone
which floats huge and purple
over her spreading hair
suspended in a shadow
that is calm
and circular.

TO N.C.G.

I had seen its approach
in the last few letters you sent
your once firm handwriting
shivering as it fell away
beyond the edge of the envelope

on the last one
you had written my name four times over
before you got it right
while some unknown hand
had filled in the address

when I opened it
only tortured hieroglyphs
harsh like my indrawn breath

I knew it was coming
but not in the afternoon   not like this

there should have been rain
the failing of light, the storm
lowering itself heavily on us
and lightning against wet window curtains
beating blindly like a bird

the phone shatters the afternoon
peeling oranges I pause
to lean lazy into the light
you always loved

the last three months
you could not stand the sun
the curtains in your room
were closed night and day
your letters written
in the dark

dark seeps through the phone now
mists pictures
so I cannot see them
swirls around plants
so they whisper darkly together
finds its freezing way
inside

I stare at my fingers
sticky-sweet   slowly drying
orange rind under nails
a blue fly
descends in a circle
to clean its legs
against my thumb

when we lay eating oranges
under a yellow Indian sky
on a terrace crumbly with moss
you began a story
of a princess with hair like monsoon clouds
in the middle
someone called you from below
you had to go

the story untold
the smell of drying oranges
in the afternoon

TERMINI

We're in an immense hall lined with black—black walls, black floor, a roof that recedes into black. A fitting end to this vacation. The smell is of steam and sweat, of fear and time running out, and barred ticket windows spilling out words that run together in jittery letters, *prenotazioni, oggetti smarriti, biglietteria.* In front of each window endless lines twist around each other. Men in black fedoras and bow-ties, girls in spiked eyelashes, stiletto heels, coats with huge black padded shoulders. Shriveled beggar-women huddled in gipsy shawls that smell of smoke. Over the entrance an enormous banner dances out *Bienvenito a Roma.* You run from line to line with your pale papery voice, from face to blank face, *Per favore, scusi, is this where I get a ticket to Venezia.* I hate the apology in your shoulderblades, your watery smile. I want to walk from your life into the yellow Roman afternoon outside, opening for me like a sunflower.

But I am trapped in my own line, a caterpillar that inches its sections up to a neon sign that announces, dispiritedly, *Ufficio Cambio.* The neon has burnt out in parts, leaving black holes in place of the 'o's, and as I watch I feel their dreadful suck at my sleeves. They siphon the air out of my lungs. They pull disheveled hair over your eyes. So that you don't see them coming, the four boys that spring out of the cement, the desperate thin bones of their hands going for your pockets, throwing you down onto the streaked floor. As through a magnifying glass I see the moving shapes of your lips, *polizia, polizia.* But a whirlwind sucks the words away and the people go on standing in their lines, the women in midnight skirts, the men in their buffed leather jackets. An elbow rammed against your breastbone, a flash as of a knife, your mouth opening like a wound. *Aiudo, aiudo.* I am trying to go to you, pushing, but they stand dense and faceless, a forest of bodies. So hard to get past them, past the cement buckling up around my feet like the years we've been together.

The boys are gone now but you're still on the floor. The lines coil past you. Gleaming Bruno Magli boots flash by, transparent Luisa Spagnoli stockings, a heart on a thin gold anklet chain. Is the roof swaying, or is it your voice? I have to bend low to hear, against your thudding heart. *Nobody tried to help, nobody even looked around.* A bruise on your forehead the color of a raincloud, the lines of your mouth smudged with disbelief. I put my arms around you and we're both shaking, the floor and walls also, they rush by us like dark glass. The letters are falling off the welcome banner onto our heads like dying stars. They sizzle in my hair. I can't brush off the burning. Is this what love is, this harsh need, this fear clamming our palms, why I can't leave you? *Let's go home,* you whisper against my shoulder. Your breath is white as the alyssums that grow in our yard. *Let's go home,* I reply.

THE REASON FOR NASTURTIUMS

All night the white fog
leans on the flattened grass,
gauzes the cherry tree,
its magenta leaves.
Nothing stirs. Not the raccoon
the two of you fed all winter. Not
the family of deer you glimpsed
last full moon lying on the deck
from the corner of your eye,
and you melting under his hot weight.
Now only his words
tumbling like drying rags
inside your smoldering skull.
You cannot breathe. You open
the back door. The world
is chill, opaque
as though a cataract had spread
milky tentacles across your eyes.
You circle the yard, blind,
until by their pungent, crushed odor
you know you are among
the nasturtiums. You kneel
in the trampled bed and touch them,
the circular silk leaves
hollowed like your hand, the petals
thin and bruised as the skin
under your eye. You sit with them
through the long dark and
in the morning you see them,
brilliant as the great red sun
pushing past the fog,
exactly the color you imagined
all night.

II

ARSON

Heat falls like rain on your shoulders,
a woman in a white suit
and heels. Or is it a child
in a torn *kameez*? Mudstains rim
your ankles, eyes. The clocks
have all stopped.
You cannot drag your eyes
from that crazed leaning, that skeleton
of smoldered, hissing brick.
Those arteries exploding in steam.
Funnels of embered iron
suck you into that burning barn
of your childhood,
your mother's screams. And then
no sounds, no sounds
except the wings that fill
the frayed, unraveling air. You've forgotten
the names and why it happens. Except
this smell of burning blood, heart-hammering.
This terrible unending crimson in the sky.

THE CHAIR

The corridor is always grey, the light a diffused welling, sourceless. Turning a sudden corner, you come upon the chair. You are fascinated by the clean white gleam of the armrests, the calm velvet of the seat. How good your back would feel, pressed against that faint lemony smell. How perfectly it would fit by your bedroom window, the one that looks out on the nasturtiums. You know the chair is not heavy. It would be easy, easy, to slide your fingers around the legs polished smooth as butter and lift it up. You reach towards the chair, its shining, and then you see you have no hands. You stare at the whitish hint of bone, the flesh puckered pink-red. The corridor walls move slowly past you, dark as tinted glass. The chair is distant now. If you looked back, you would see it glowing faintly, an enamelled miniature. You bring the stumps close to your face, almost to touching. You try to remember how it happened. After a while you will let them drop to your side, resume walking. And when, turning a sudden corner, you come upon the chair again, you will not recognize it.

MAGRITTE KNEW

that inside each woman
square and blue
at the very center
of the chest
hangs a window
where clouds billow
damp and white
like lungs
breathing the sky
where on a winter afternoon
five Canadian geese.
in a frenzy of black wings
spearhead directly
into a falling sun
and where
after they are gone
night loops
the silent runners
of the trumpetvine
its bells of orange light
glowing into our dark

MRS. A. AT THE FRUIT MARKET

The peaches beckon to her,
soft gold curves, luscious
Titian flesh.
Under her faltering finger
the velvet skin
is fuzzy
like a youth's first beard.

But she finally moves on to the apples
roundly solid, crunchy-clean
when bitten into
so much more suitable
for a woman living alone.
Double-wrapped in plastic
they will keep
for weeks in the refrigerator.

At the checkstand
she takes off her glasses, rubs
at the edges of her eyes,
the growing cracks.
Behind her the piled pomegranates
have split open, spilling crystal pink
like smiling untasted mouths.

THE TOURISTS

The heat is like a fist between the eyes. The man and woman wander down a narrow street of flies and stray cats looking for the Caracalla Baths. The woman wears a cotton dress embroidered Mexican style with bright flowers. The man wears Rayban glasses and knee-length shorts. They wipe at the sweat with white handkerchiefs because they have used up all the kleenex they brought.

The woman is afraid they are lost. She holds on tightly to the man's elbow and presses her purse into her body. The purse is red leather, very new, bought by him outside the Coliseum after a half-hour of earnest bargaining. She wonders what they are doing in this airless alley with the odor of stale urine rising all around them, what they are doing in Rome, what they are doing in Europe. The man tries to walk tall and confident, shoulders lifted, but she can tell he is nervous about the youths in tight levis lounging against the fountain, eyeing, he thinks, their Leica. In his halting guidebook Italian he asks the passers-by—there aren't many because of the heat—*Dov'e terme di Caracalla?* and then, *Dov'e la stazione?* but they stare at him and do not seem to understand.

The woman is tired. It distresses her to not know where she is, to have to trust herself to the truths of strangers, their indecipherable mouths, their quick eyes, their fingers each pointing in a different direction, *eccolo, il treno per Milano, la torre pendente, la cattedrale, il palazzo ducale.* She wants to go to the bathroom, to get a drink, to find a taxi. She asks if it is O.K. to wash her face in the fountain, but he shakes his head. It's not hygenic, and besides, a man with a pock-marked face and black teeth has been watching them from a doorway, and he wants to get out of the alley as soon as he can.

The woman sighs, gets out a crumpled tour brochure from her purse and fans herself and then him with it. They are walking faster now, she stumbling a bit in her sandals. She wishes they were back in the hotel or better still in her own cool garden. She is sure that in her absence the Niles Lilies are dying, in spite of the automatic sprinkler system, and the gophers have taken over the lawn. Is it worth it, even for the colors in the Sistine chapel, the curve of Venus' throat as she rises from the sea? The green statue of the boy with the goose among the rosemary in a Pompeii courtyard? She makes a mental note to pick up some gopher poison on the way back from the airport. They turn a corner onto a broader street. Surely this is the one that will lead them back to the Circo Massimo and the subway. The man lets out a deep breath, starts to smile. Then suddenly, footsteps, a quick clattering on the cobbles behind. They both stiffen, remembering. Yesterday one of the tourists in their hotel was mugged outside the Villa Borghesi. Maybe they should have taken the bus tour after all. He tightens his hands into fists, his face into a scowl. Turns. But it is only a dog, its pink tongue hanging, its ribs sticking out of its scabby coat. It stops and observes them, wary, ready for flight. Then the woman touches his hand. *Look, look.* From where they are standing they can see into someone's backyard. Sheets and pillowcases drying whitely in the sun, a palm scattering shade over blocks of marble from a broken column, a big bougainvillea that covers the crumbling wall. A breeze comes up, lifting their hair. Sudden smell of rain. They stand there, man and woman and dog, watching the bright purple flowers tumble over the broken bricks.

THE BLUE ROOM

In the blue room
it is always raining.
After a while you get used
to the perpetually sodden skin,
the puckered fingers.
You no longer notice
how your soaked clothes
weigh you down.

You trail through pools of color
which are the days,
which sometimes leave
a streak, grey, or a pale orange,
on your leg. Somewhere above
pain closes around the light
like a fist.

In the blue room
you learn to breathe
through water.
You cup in your dark hands,
like bubbles,
the fragile words
you have always loved.
When they start breaking,
you learn
to open the fingers,
each porous, polished bone.

LEROY AT THE ZOO

unlike the other children
is not intrigued
by the squirrel monkey's antics.
The grunts of a pair of fighting camels
do not excite him.
In front of the African compound
he ignores me as I point
to gazelles and giraffes,
rummages in the picnic basket
for an apple which later
he will throw, half-eaten
into the elephant's enclosure
when the keeper is not looking.

In the children's section
he pokes half-hearted at a turtle's face
then clambers onto its
cracked-earth shell where someone
has neatly stenciled, "Keep Off."
He watches the others petting the goats —
father, mother, the white-hooved kids —
and shakes his head when I call him
to them. Abandoned
in a shopping mall at five, he is
no believer in happy families.

Near the snakes his eyes still.
He presses his face against the cage
and the Burmese Python slithers
its long white belly along the glass
and flicks its tongue at him. I point out
discarded scraps of snakeskin
near the water-trough. Leroy looks,
silent. Streetwise at eight, he does not think
dusty brown can be shrugged off,
at will, for shiny checkered gold.

On the way back he sleeps,
his head against the window,
a black unpetalled sunflower.
Driving the highway of parched oleanders
I dream him running in tall grass
under a morning sky.
When he raises his arms, his old skin
splits down the sides, slides off,
leaves him wet and gleaming.
The red sun dries him. Gold poppies
call him his new name.

NIGHT SEA, NIGHT SKY

Cozumel sunset. Our boat cleaving
                through a sea like blood
      rattling scuba gear.
The chugging motor stops.
              Night, and the thick swish
of inky water, warm as skin.
      It parts, then folds itself
around our bodies
          eager as a lover.

     We sink and sink.
  Shoals of tiny Astyanax
          flit between our legs
      flecks of silver light.
          Mollienisia, velvet brown
    their fins a lazy brush
of lace across my face.

Then the hull of the wreck
         spiking upward sudden
      black in the now-green water.
        Crusty canker growths
break off and molder in my fingers.
      Everywhere ropy tentacles of seaweed
      and in the yawning dark below
    a slight movement, a gleam like eyes.
    I tug at your reluctant shoulder
        till we start back.

Rising with bubbles
dimly phosphorescent
in quivering underwater light I see
an enormous blueness plummet down on us
blunt silhouette
of a huge flat head
and thrash out
but the water coils around
pounds in my ears, holds me down.
I see you gesture wildly
mouthing through your mask
close my eyes
wait for teeth.

Instead, sleek rush of skin
against my belly
nudge of a mouth
smiling its wide dolphin smile
and inches away from mine
his unwinking eye
holding me in bright blackness.

He rises with us all the way
touching me, then you.
When I put out my hands
his body is a ripple
like water in wind.
From the boat
we turn to watch. He leaps
in moonlight, gleaming
then is gone.

All the way back
inside me, the night sky
is filled
with the flash of dolphins
their skins like blue pearl
leaping again
and again.

DEAF CHILD AT SEASHORE

At the white edge of water
the back of her head
alone, unmoving,
glints like a wet black shell.
Gulls wheel in a red-beaked, cryless net
over this, her first ocean
foaming and salt-silent.
She watches the fat underwater
roll of kelp, dim green,
forever shifting shape
like the mouths of the children
who play tag in the waves.

She waits. When the surf
has quenched the low sun
and she is with herself
in dark, she will step down
to water. By the light
in her bones she will
see it sing. When the dolphins
come in answer
she will somersault with them
into a star-splintering dance.
Like them she will laugh and laugh
without sound.

SKIN

I woke this morning with a tingly feeling all over my body, not unpleasant, kind of like it feels between your teeth after you've poked at your gum with something for a while, and when I looked I discovered I had no skin. I was disconcerted for a moment, but not really upset, not like someone else would have been. My skin has been nothing but a source of trouble for me ever since the midwife announced to my mother that not only was it a girlchild, but it was also the color of a mud-road in the monsoon. Mother refused to look, and all through the weeks she had to breastfeed me she kept her head turned away, so all I remember of her is a smooth creamy earlobe with a gold loop dangling from it.

I spent my childhood learning to blend in with the furniture, which wasn't too difficult since the heavy mahogany was a perfect match for my skin, and after my marriage I had ample opportunity to perfect the skill. That I got married at all was a miracle, as I was a far cry from the milk-and-honey shade that mother-in-laws are always looking for. Relatives ascribed my great good luck to temporary insanity on the part of my in-laws, probably brought about by something my desperate parents slipped into their rosewater syrup when they came to view me. Or perhaps it was the substantial dowry my father paid in order to get rid of me—not too unhappily, for as everyone knows, a grown daughter in the house is worse than a firebrand in the grainstacks.

My in-laws quickly returned to normal, and the morning after the wedding I was sent to the kitchen. There, camouflaged by the smoke-streaked walls, I cooked enormous breakfasts, lunches and dinners, with tea twice in between, for the family and all their guests that I never saw. I only came to my husband's bedroom after the lights were out so he didn't have to look at me, and when he had been satisfied I returned to my quarters. So you can understand why I'm intrigued rather than dismayed as I gingerly touch my arm.

It doesn't hurt, not too much. There's no mirror in the pantry where I sleep, so I can't see my face, but I take a good look at everything else—fingers and elbows, ankles and calves, the soles of my feet. All is a delicate uniform pink, kind of like the inside of a baby's mouth, no, paler, more like the flesh of a *hilsa* fish after you've sliced it open. I'm so fascinated I do something I've never done before—I remove my clothes and examine the forbidden parts—mounds, hollows, slits. I notice the veins and arteries below the surface, red and blue skeins of pulsing silk, the translucent glistening tissues along the curves.

How beautiful I am! I can't wait to share my new body with my family. Surely they will be proud of me, love me at last, a daughter-in-law to brag about, to show off to strangers. I try to imagine the smile on my husband's face, a bit difficult as it's something I've never seen, and on an impulse I rummage in the chest till I find my marriage sari, a lovely deep silk, purple-red. I'd heard a wedding guest say that it made me look like an eggplant. But now I pull it out and arrange it around my hips and shoulders with excited fingers. How my skinless body glows against it! How proudly my breasts push against the fabric!

Ready now, I stand tall. I picture myself sweeping into the great hall, the awe on their faces, the adoration. I practice my words of forgiveness, my gracious smile. And then, with my hand stretched out to turn the knob, I notice it. The door is gone. The door to my room is gone.

I look for it everywhere, feeling the cracked, peeling whitewash, the bricks that scrape my new fingertips raw. I move faster, searching, my breath coming in gasps. It's a trick, a new cruel trick, the latest in the series, but I won't be taken in by it. I throw myself against the wall, hammer at it. Shout. The sound falls back into my ears, small, like a cry from the bottom of a well-shaft. But I won't give up. I *know* it's there, somewhere, my door. I won't be kept from it.

THE RETURN

I come back to the house
only when I'm sure you have left.
I am not surprised to find
you've taken all the mirrors,
even the cracked one
in the bathroom.
It's a little disconcerting
to discover that you've also
taken the window-shades,
but it doesn't really matter because
you've taken the windows as well.
I turn to leave and find
the door, too, is gone
with its long blue shadow.

I stand in the middle of the empty house.
The walls begin to walk inward.
When they touch me I see
they are painted with the dark
rich smells of your body.

III

THE SNAKE CHARMERS

The snake charmers are always male.
They have no homes. Their skin
is bluish-brown, from snakebites
or lack of baths. Like night fog
under the river-banyan
their footsteps make no sound.

From their shoulders swing
twin wicker baskets, in each
a hundred snakes. The domed lids
woven with mandrake root
and magic keep the snakes asleep.
They never eat, only drink
milk from red earthen bowls,
like their snakes.

On their backs they carry
enormous patched bags.
Sometimes from inside them
you hear a child cry.

Cloudy evenings at the bazaar's edge
they play on gourd flutes
shaped like beetroots.
The wicker lids open. The snakes
rise up: black lightning cobras
anacondas checkered gold
the squash-vine snake, whiplash-thin
dripping green poison.

The snake charmers sway, hands
fisted around magic feathers.
The snakes coil around them.
Some dance. The anaconda
opens its huge saw-toothed jaws
and takes in an arm elbow-deep.

The crowd gasps. The snake charmers smile
thin smiles like knives.
But all the while
with eyes like sunken stars
they are searching the crowd
for a boychild, alone.
When they see him
they make a secret sign
and the child must follow them
into the evening
into the tall river grasses.

If he is clever
with strong, white teeth
they teach him their secrets.
If he cries or is crosseyed
they sprinkle him with black
snakeroot powder. His limbs
pull in, his head grows long and flat
his skin sprouts scales. All night
they make him dance
to the high, hollow sound
of their flutes.

When the sun rises, the snake charmers
disappear
into holes or dreams.

ON DHARMATALA STREET

The pavements have disappeared
under the muscled brown rush
of the April rains.
The roadside vendors
cover their wicker baskets
of puffed rice and chilies
and start home. The trams
have all stopped running.
The school across the street
opens its gates early, and

boys in red shorts dart out,
hands cupping paper boats
like flames. Their bare legs
are ringed with dark water, their cries
rise through the rain
like birds. Next door
someone is frying onion pakoras,
and the smell
curls itself around the balcony

where I stand, watching
clouds like steel wool
rub against rooftops,
waiting for you
to take the steps two at a time,
pants rolled to your knees,
shoes in your hand,
rain-wet lips tasting like
this sudden light in the sky.

TO MRINAL SEN, ON SEEING HIS FILM *BHUVAN SHOME*

Like Bhuvan Shome,
we stand surprised,
in our hands the trembling
moist weight, the bird
we have hunted down

The man wanted to shoot birds.
So you brought him
to the heart of the land.
In rural Gujarat
you faced him with the silver flight
of wild ducks across dunes
vast beyond human crossing.
The rush of their beating wings
took his breath
so that he could not pull the trigger,
almost.

It is easy to lose oneself
lying still on the sands,
eyes wrinkled against the grit
of constant wind,
watching clouds
progress across the sky
with endless amoeba movements
while one waits for the birds.
In that world
where always beyond the last dune
rises another
between oneself and the sea,
time is a feathered flash
falling in midair,
its sharp thin cry
cut off by the dull thud
of body hitting ground,
the tread of one's feet
ankle-deep in sand
lumbering relentless towards
those frantic eyes.

VOICES FOR A RIVER RISING

1 *
On the other shore of the river
I see the lamplight in my mother's door,
smell the basil plant.
Brother, o brother,
my heart will not let me be.
Sister, dear sister,
stay another month
in your in-laws' house,
soon I will bring a palanquin
to fetch you home.
My bones are roasted with sorrow,
my flesh is roped with grief.
River, o river water,
rise that I may leap into you.

2.
The first to know were the cows
crying all day in the barn,
lifting long white throats
to the sky. Could they feel
through their unquiet hooves the shudder
of the land under a black wall
of water? Before the river's roar
shook us from sleep
they broke their ropes and fled.
But where could they go? The water
took them, every one.

3.
I tell you I saw them the night before,
where the tamarind tree
leans into swirling water.
They were all there —
the boatman's boy, Kesto's wife,
your Haru, my own Manik —
all lost in the last flood.
But young, so young in the white moon.
Their mouths shone with foam.
In their hair, waterlilies.
In their calling hands.

4*
O river friend,
from which land have you come,
when will your roaming end,
o friend river?
You destroy one bank, then
build another
tell me, o river,
what can you do to me
whose life has lost its banks?
O river friend.

5.
Waking, I knew it was already too late.
It filled my nose and mouth,
crushed my chest, flung me into winds
shrieking in my daughter's voice.
All was gone. The hut, my people,
the ricefields that sang me asleep.
I let the water take me. But then,
rough bristles against my sinking body,
the black boar swimming with the tide,
snout skyward, its great tusks
gleaming. It spoke and I obeyed.
Clasped its neck. And all turned silver,
silver. O I would once more
risk death to see the shining
in the eyes of my boar brother.

6.
They ignore the old songs
which call me goddess, destroyer
of men's deeds. Again they lie
in my lap to sleep. Scratch seeds
into my flanks to grow unruly weeds.
And cry when I wash them clean.
Men's nature is to forget and sow
and weep. Mine to rise up. To sweep.

7*
Under the river lie the bones,
the shining bones. The bones roll white
with the tide and they sing.
In the middle of the river
rises an island.
There the merchant rests
his peacock-throated boat.
O fill his boat with sweet white rice,
bananas shining gold,
bananas and rice
growing from our flesh.

8.
The morning after, the brown water
still rising, and we survivors
huddling on the verandah, watching
the swirling carcasses, wondering how soon
the vultures would come, and the plague.
Abinash rowed up in an old dinghy
he had found somewhere. Pointed where
the tide was snatching at the leafless banyan.
See those people hanging
onto the branches?
They'll be swept away
unless we do something. Sure death,
we told him, to go into the mouth
of the she-devil in that little boat.
But he shook his head
in that stubborn way and plunged in.
Well, the water caught him soon enough,
dragged him to the banyan. But seeing the boat
they lost their heads and
in spite of what he shouted
jumped in all at once. The dinghy sank,
of course. We saw it all —
a few flailing hands, some cries,
a broken, spinning oar.
What could we do? The water took them all.
Only his red headgear
caught in the banyan branches.
See where it hangs, faded remains
of a man, of a river rising.

* adapted from Bengali folk songs

THE COMB, OR AN INDIAN FAIRYTALE

The princess
is always combing
hair like monsoon clouds
with an ivory comb.

Its jewel eyes alert her
to the approach of brigands
with nefarious designs.

Only the prince
whom the wicked stepmother
has changed into an ape
can shuffle up with his
drunken-sailor gait
and pluck it from her
while she is still laughing
with her pomegranate mouth.

The comb twists and struggles,
tries to sink its needle teeth
into his wrist.
But the ape-prince, forewarned
has it firmly
in his hairy, tensile grip.

The princess must now follow him
meekly in her bride-red silks
to his ship. If her tendriled hair
swells about her face
like a monsoon,
no one remarks on it.

The comb closes its eyes
and dreams of dark
when it will thrust
its ivory fangs
into a hirsute neck
and return, hand in hand
with the princess, their path
strewn with pomegranate flowers.

The ship sets sail. Wedding lamps
wink like jewel eyes. Shehnai music
swells the silken banners.
The ape-prince and his bride
spend a night of joy
in the nuptial chamber. If
there are noises, they
are drowned by firecrackers
exploding like the hearts
of pomegranates.

In the morning they emerge
hand in hand, her hair
neatly braided and the prince
human
gleaming like ivory.

No mention is made of the comb.

INDIGO

Bengal, 1779-1859

The fields flame with it, endless, blue
as cobra poison. It has entered
our blood and pulses
up our veins like night. There is
no other color. The planter's whip
splits open the flesh of our faces,
a blue liquid light trickles
through the fingers. Blue dyes the lungs
when we breathe. Only the obstinate eyes

refuse to forget where once the rice
parted the earth's moist skin
and pushed up reed by reed,
green, then rippled gold
like the Arhiyal's waves. Stitched
into our eyelids, the broken dark,
the torches of the planter's men,
fire walling like a tidal wave that
flattened the ripe grain with a smell
like charred flesh, broke
on our huts. And the wind
screaming in the voices of women
dragged to the plantation,
feet, hair, torn breasts.

In the worksheds, we dip our hands,
their violent forever blue,
in the dye, pack it
in great embossed chests
for the East India Company.
Our ankles gleam thin blue
from the chains. After that night
many of the women killed
themselves. Drowning
was the easiest.
Sometimes the Arhiyal gave us back
the naked, bloated bodies, the faces
eaten by fish. We hold on

to red, the color
of their saris, the marriage mark
on their foreheads,
we hold it carefully inside
our blue skulls, like a man
in the cold *Paush* night
holds in his cupped palms
a spark, its welcome scorch,
feeds it his foggy breath
till he can set it down
in the right place,
to blaze up and burst
like the hot heart of a star
over the whole horizon,
a burning so beautiful you want it
to never end.

Note: Indigo planting was forced on the farmers of Bengal, India, by the British, who exported it as a cash crop for almost a hundred years until the peasant uprising of 1860, when the plantations were destroyed.

BOWBAJAR MORH

As she turns the corner
of Bowbajar Morh,
they break on her ear —
so many bells.
From the white Shiva temple,
its trident spearing the hot noon.
From the cream-and-red tram
skirting the crowd,
on its side *Jabakusum oil*
for hair like rain-clouds.
From the old, cracked
throat of the green-coconut seller,
the great globed fruits hanging
from his shoulders
as from a tree.
His tongue rings out their coolness
in such pure tones
that she calls him

as he's crossing the street.
He turns. And at that moment
the hurtling taxi   in a green
explosion of coconuts
the distinct thwack of his head
on concrete. Instant bloom
of blood   so much blood
his chest   shoulders   his torn
dhoti. And the crowd roiling
crazed with bloodscent.
She starts to run to him

but her friend grips her, hard.
He knows Calcutta crowds.
Already they've dragged out
the driver   a fist
stamps out his mouth
his eye
blood spurts in the hot
white light as from nowhere.

She knows that salt taste
as he falls and the bloods
soak the asphalt the same red
as the clanging police bells.
Her friend thrusts her

into a narrow alley.
The alley of flowers
damp cool stalls
misted with petal breath
where old men regard her
with the eyes
of the coconut seller
as they braid
gardenias and jasmines
with silver cords for weddings,
and for funerals
thick garlands of snowy *bel*
to lay over the silent
sheeted dead.
The faint ringing of roses
the tolling of pallbearers
all the way
to the cremation ghats,
tightening around her so she
cannot breathe, crimson and thorned,
this blinding rope of bells.

THE TEA BOY

after Mira Nair's film **Salaam Bombay!**

All day I carry glasses of tea
down streets
full of holes or feet
waiting to trip me. Above
summer is singeing the feathers
of black pigeons
        that circle and circle.
                Gopi carries a knife
                with a twisted snake handle.
            Each time a glass breaks
            Chacha cuts my pay.
Dark windows.
Women with satin eyes
calling me. The tea
thick and sweet
in its rippling brown skin.
        Downstairs pimps play cards
           all morning. Sometimes I take
           a sip from each glass
           when no one is watching.
                    Broken-horned cow
                    chewing garbage
in the alley where we sleep. Rain
soaks my yellow shirt,
turns the tea salt.
        Cinnamon smell
        of women's brown bodies. When
        you can't stand any more
        the pavement is soft enough.
I am hiding my money
behind a loose brick
in the bridge-wall.   First thing to learn: melt
           into pavement
        when you hear police vans.
                Skin doesn't want

                                        to hold in all the bones.
                        Chillum sells hashish
                        to tourists
by India Gate. It pulls you
out of your body, flings you
into the sun. The night Gopi
mugged the old man
he bought us all *parathas*
at Bansi's Corner Restaurant.
                        Footsteps following me,
                        a muffled cough. My soles
                        turning to stone.

                                        Lie down.
                                        Night-dust
warm as Shiva's ashes. When
I have five hundred rupees
I can go back
to my mother in Bijapur.
                        Till I fall asleep I watch
                        that fierce glistening
                        the sky full of scars.

TRAIN

Every evening between six and seven I go to Sialdah Station. No one knows about this. Not even my wife, for how would I explain it to her? It isn't as though anybody ever comes to visit me. Nor do I travel anywhere. And if I told her that it was a good way of avoiding the rush-hour buses, she would know right away, as she always does, that I was lying.

I never go all the way inside where you need a platform ticket. A platform ticket costs two rupees, and she keeps track of every paisa of my salary. But it doesn't matter because from behind the iron railings I can still see and hear it all: coolies in red uniforms and polished brass armlets carrying enormous khaki holdalls on their heads; vendors pushing wooden carts stacked with everything from yellow Mausambi fruit to the latest film magazines with Amitabha on the cover; newspaper boys crying *Amrita Bajaar, Amrita Bajaar;* the departure announcements, thick with static; the tolling of the station clock whose minute-hand moves in slow heavy jerks. And then suddenly everything is drowned in the shriek of an incoming train.

This is my favorite moment, when a train pulls slowly into the station, the engine's black cylinder sweating, the wheels' chugging rhythm cut off by the hiss of brakes. The smoke billows out one last time over the waiting faces on the platform. A whistle shrills, the doors open, and a man in dark glasses swings down from the first class compartment, a Pan Am flight bag slung casually from his shoulder. Someone in a sun-colored rayon shirt helps a laughing young woman down the steps, his hand on her bare upper arm. Her salwar-kameez is printed with orange butterflies that flutter as they race towards the gates. The clock strikes seven. A coolie shoves past me, swearing. A spat-out wad of betel leaf spatters my pant leg. I remember that my wife has told me to be sure to bring the cough mixture for the baby.

At night I lie in the airless bedroom that smells of diapers and her hair oil. If I stretch out my hand, I will encounter the dark shape of her body. I know she is waiting and will not protest if I climb on top, as long as I don't wake the baby. The streetlight has thrown the shadow of the windowbars against the peeling wall. They look a little like railroad tracks. I lie chewing the inside of my cheek, its salty taste, to hold down the spiralling, like smoke inside my throat. If I stay very, very still, surely her breath will slow into sleep. Somewhere the night trains are flying across glistening tracks, their headlights spearing the dark. And suddenly it comes to me again, that pounding hot magic smell of iron and steam and speed. I remember that tomorrow evening the Pathankot Express arrives at 6:45, and I don't mind too much when my wife turns and pulls me to her with damp hands.

WOMAN WITH KITE

Meadow of crabgrass, faded dandelions,
querulous child-voices. She takes
from her son's disgruntled hands the spool
of a kite that will not fly. Pulls
on the heavy string, ground-glass rough
between her thumb and finger. Feels the kite,
translucent purple square, rise
in a resistant arc, flapping
against the wind. Kicks off her *chappals,*
tucks up her *kurta* so she can
run with it, light
flecking off her hair as when she was
sexless-young. Up, up

past the puff-cheeked clouds, she
follows it, her eyes slit-smiling
at the sun. She has forgotten
her tugging children, their *give me,*
give me wails. She sprints
backwards, sure-footed, she cannot
fall, connected to the air, she
is flying, the wind blows through her, takes
her red *dupatta,* mark of marriage.
And she laughs like a woman
should never laugh

so the two widows on the park bench
stare and huddle their white-veiled heads
to gossip-whisper. The children
have fallen, breathless,
in the grass behind. She
laughs like wild water, shaking
her braids loose, she laughs
like a fire, the spool a blur
between her hands, the string
unraveling all the way
to release it into space, her life,
into its bright, weightless orbit.

Chitra Banerjee Divakaruni lives in the San Francisco Bay Area with her husband and teaches at Foothill College, where she is a director for the annual National Creative Writing Conference. Her poems, short stories and translations have appeared in numerous magazines and anthologies in India and the U.S.A. Her first book of poetry, *Dark Like the River*, was published by Writers Workshop Press, India, 1987. She was nominated for the Pushcart Prize in 1989.

SMCL

3 5151 00206 0994

BOOKS FROM THE BERKELEY POETS WORKSHOP & PRESS

BERKELEY POETS COOPERATIVE ANTHOLOGY
 1970-1980, poetry and fiction, 275 pages, $6.95
SHE COMES WHEN YOU'RE LEAVING by Bruce Boston
 fiction, 64 pages, $5.95
UNFREE ASSOCIATIONS by Michael Covino
 poetry, 64 pages, $5.95
SELF-PORTRAIT WITH HAND MICROSCOPE by Lucille Day
 poetry, 64 pages, $5.95
NEWSPAPER STORIES by Patricia Dienstfrey
 poetry, 64 pages, $5.95
IN THIS HOUR by Charles Entrekin
 poetry, 80 pages, $6.95
HALF A BOTTLE OF CATSUP by Ted Fleischman
 poetry, 36 pages, $5.95
HEAR MY STORY by Dennis Folly
 poetry, 48 pages, $5.95
PERCEPTION BARRIERS by Robert Frazier
 poetry, 48 pages, $5.95
THE GHOST OF THE BUICK by Bruce Hawkins
 poetry, 48 pages, $5.95
INSTEAD OF A CAMERA by Carla Kandinsky
 poetry, 48 pages, $5.95
DANCING AT GROUND ZERO by Gerald Jorge Lee
 poetry, 48 pages, $5.95
THE IMPOSSIBILITY OF REDEMPTION
IS SOMETHING WE HADN'T COUNTED ON by Linda Watanabe McFerrin
 poetry, 64 pages, $5.95
WASH ME ON HOME, MAMA by Peter Najarian
 fiction, 84 pages, $5.95
ONCE MORE OUT OF DARKNESS by Alicia Ostriker
 poetry, 32 pages, $5.95
JOHN DANCED by Gail Rudd
 poetry, 32 pages, $5.95
TRUANT BATHER by Mark Taksa
 poetry, 48 pages, $5.95
THE MACHINE SHUTS DOWN by Rod Tulloss
 poetry, 40 pages, $5.95
BY PARKED CARS by J.D. Woolery
 poetry, 48 pages, $5.95